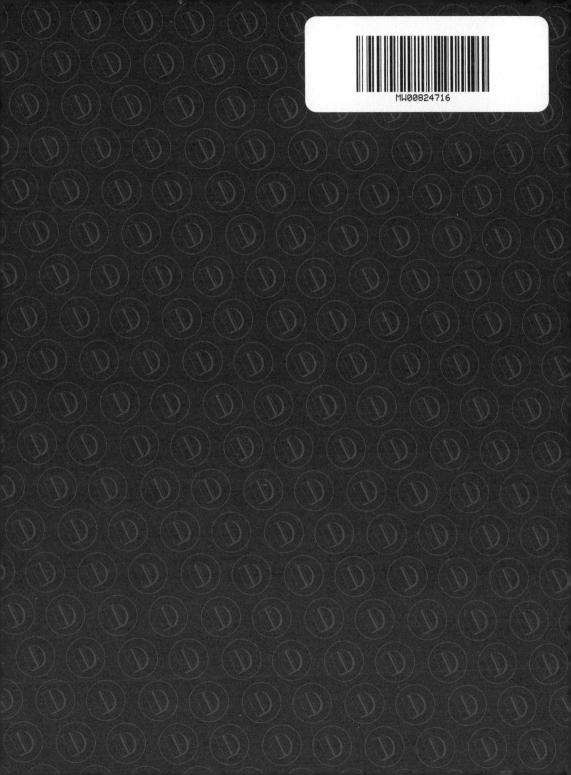

DUMPLINGS

DUMPLINGS

LA TAVERNE DE ZHAO
PHOTOGRAPHY BY SHAKTHI PEIRIS SAMANAKKODI
ILLUSTRATIONS BY VALENTINE FERRANDI

Smith
Street
Books

CONTENTS

14

PORK & SAUERKRAUT

16

SICHUAN

18

BEEF & ONION

20

LAMB & CARROT

22

VEGETARIAN

26

PORK & CORN

28

CRYSTAL PRAWN

30

SEAFOOD

32

FOUR-FLAVOUR

34

BEEF

36

CHICKEN

40

HENAN

42

SHANGHAI

44

NANJING

46

GOLDEN FISH

48

CABBAGE & TOFU

50

PORK & PRAWN

54

EGG DUMPLING SOUP

56

SHAANXI DUMPLING SOUP

58

TINY DUMPLING SOUP

60

VEGETABLE DUMPLING SOUP

62

BEEF DUMPLING SOUP

INGREDIENTS

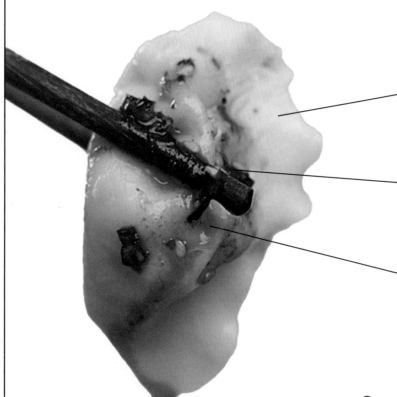

Dumpling dough

*Filling, made from
chopped meat, seafood
or vegetables*

Dipping sauce

BEST SERVED

Dumplings are best eaten
on the day they are made.

They can be frozen.

HELPFUL TOOLS

• Large bowl • Wooden spoon or spatula
• Sharp knife • Rolling pin • Chopping board
• Saucepan • Steamer basket • Frying pan
• Slotted spoon • Chopsticks • Serving plates
and bowls

DUMPLING TUTORIAL

IN 4 STEPS

1 Prepare the dough.

2 Prepare the filling.

3 Fill and fold the dumplings.

4 Cook the dumplings by steaming, boiling or frying.

DUMPLING DOUGH

MAKES 30 DUMPLINGS	
PREP 10 MINUTES	
REST 15 MINUTES	

*420 g (15 oz) plain (all-purpose) flour
240 ml (8 fl oz) water*

1 Combine the flour and water in a large bowl. Using a wooden spoon or spatula, mix until well combined.

2 Tip the dough onto a clean work surface and knead by hand for a few minutes.

3 Form the dough into a neat ball and place in a clean bowl. Cover and allow to rest for 15 minutes.

4 After the dough has rested, roll it into long strips.

5 Use a knife to cut the dough into 10 g (¼ oz) pieces.

6 Use a rolling pin to roll out each piece of dough into a 7–8 cm (2¾–3¼ in) disc to make a dumpling wrapper.

HOT DUMPLING DOUGH
(ideal for steamed dumplings)

PREP 10 MINUTES **REST** 40 MINUTES
• *240 g (8½ oz) plain (all-purpose) flour* • *40 g (⅓ cup) cornflour (cornstarch)*
• *2 teaspoons neutral-flavoured oil*

Combine the ingredients in a large bowl and pour in 180 ml (6 fl oz) boiling water. Once the water has cooled to a manageable temperature, bring the dough together, transfer to a clean work surface and knead until well combined, then allow to rest for 40 minutes. Roll the dough into long strips, cut into 10 g (¼ oz) pieces and roll into 7–8 cm (2¾–3¼ in) discs. Cover with plastic wrap and refrigerate before use.

THE DIFFERENT FOLDS

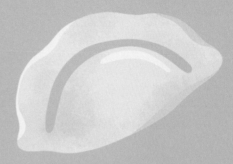

HALF-MOON
DUMPLINGS

1 Place 20 g (¾ oz) filling in the centre of a dumpling wrapper.

2 Fold the dumpling in half and bring the edges together.

3 Use your thumbs and index fingers to delicately push the filling to the centre of the dumpling.

4 Using your thumb and index finger, firmly press the edges of the dumpling wrapper together to seal the filling inside.

PLEATED
DUMPLINGS

1 Place 20g (¾ oz) filling in the centre of a dumpling wrapper, holding it with the thumb and index finger of your left hand.

2 Pinch the right corner of the dumpling together with your right index finger and thumb.

3 Continue to pinch pleats all the way along the edge.

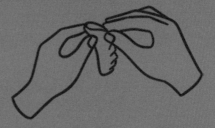

4 Firmly seal the dough to stop the dumpling opening during cooking.

THE DIFFERENT FOLDS

SOUP
DUMPLINGS

1 Place 20 g (¾ oz) filling in the centre of a dumpling wrapper, holding it in your left hand, and fold the dumpling in half.

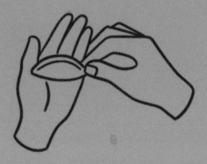

2 Seal the edges of the dumpling wrapper with the index finger and thumb of your right hand.

3 Bring the two ends in towards each other, to form a circle.

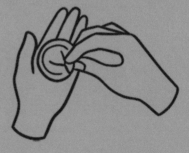

4 Pinch the two ends closed, so the dumpling takes the shape of a circle.

FOUR-FLAVOUR DUMPLINGS

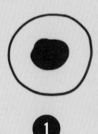

1

Place 15 g (½ oz) filling in the centre of a dumpling wrapper.

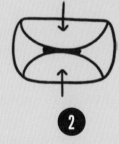

2

Fold the top and bottom halves over and firmly pinch the ends together.

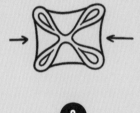

3

Fold the short sides in half and pinch the ends firmly in the middle.

4

Form four hollows with your fingers.

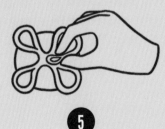

5

Pinch the middle edges of the hollows firmly together.

6

Fill the dumpling hollows with your prepared toppings.

Pork & sauerkraut

MAKES 30 DUMPLINGS

PREP 30 MINUTES

COOK 20 MINUTES

350 g (12½ oz) minced (ground) pork

1 tablespoon finely chopped chives

1½ teaspoons finely chopped fresh ginger

1½ teaspoons salt

½ teaspoon MSG

20 ml (¾ fl oz) neutral-flavoured oil

50 ml (1¾ fl oz) water

250 g (9 oz) sauerkraut

1 PREPARE THE DOUGH

Prepare the dough following the instructions on page 8.

2 PREPARE THE FILLING

Place the meat in a large bowl, breaking it up a bit with a wooden spoon or chopsticks. Add the chives, ginger, salt, MSG, oil and water. Mix vigorously in the same direction until well combined and sticky.

Drain the sauerkraut, cut it into small pieces, add to the pork and continue mixing until well combined.

3 FILL AND FOLD THE DUMPLINGS

Divide the filling among the dumpling wrappers in 20 g (¾ oz) portions and fold following the instructions on page 10 or 11.

4 BOIL THE DUMPLINGS

Bring a large saucepan of water to the boil and add 15 dumplings. Wait for the water to come back up to the boil, then add 15 ml (½ fl oz) cold water. Repeat this process twice. While cooking, gently stir the dumplings to stop them sticking together. When they float to the surface, they are ready. Scoop out the dumplings with a slotted spoon and serve hot.

Cook the remaining dumplings in the same way.

Sichuan

MAKES 30 DUMPLINGS

PREP 30 MINUTES

COOK 20 MINUTES

Filling

600 g (1 lb 5 oz) minced (ground) pork

2 teaspoons light soy sauce

1¾ teaspoons salt

1 teaspoon sesame oil

½ teaspoon MSG

½ teaspoon ground white pepper

100 ml (3½ fl oz) water

For serving

30 ml (1 fl oz) chilli oil

chopped coriander (cilantro)

chopped chives

crushed peanuts

sesame seeds

① PREPARE THE DOUGH

Prepare the dough following the instructions on page 8.

② PREPARE THE FILLING

Place the meat in a large bowl, breaking it up a bit with a wooden spoon or chopsticks. Add the remaining ingredients. Mix vigorously in the same direction until well combined and sticky.

③ FILL AND FOLD THE DUMPLINGS

Divide the filling among the dumpling wrappers in 20 g (¾ oz) portions and fold following the instructions on page 10 or 11.

④ BOIL THE DUMPLINGS

Bring a large saucepan of water to the boil and add 15 dumplings. Wait for the water to come back up to the boil, then add 15 ml (½ fl oz) cold water. Repeat this process twice. While cooking, gently stir the dumplings to stop them sticking together. When they float to the surface, they are ready. Scoop out the dumplings with a slotted spoon and serve hot, with chilli oil, coriander, chives, crushed peanuts and sesame seeds.

Cook the remaining dumplings in the same way.

Beef & onion

MAKES 30 DUMPLINGS

MAKES 30 DUMPLINGS

PREP 30 MINUTES

COOK 20 MINUTES

400 g (14 oz) minced (ground) beef (20% fat or higher)

150 g (1 cup) finely diced onion

100 g (⅔ cup) grated carrot

20 ml (¾ fl oz) light soy sauce

1¼ teaspoons sugar

1½ teaspoons salt

¾ teaspoon MSG

½ teaspoon Chinese five-spice

½ teaspoon ground white pepper

100 ml (3½ fl oz) water

15 ml (½ fl oz) sesame oil

15 ml (½ fl oz) neutral-flavoured oil

① PREPARE THE DOUGH

Prepare the dough following the instructions on page 8.

② PREPARE THE FILLING

Place the meat in a large bowl, breaking it up a bit with a wooden spoon or chopsticks. Add the remaining ingredients, except the sesame and neutral-flavoured oil. Mix vigorously in the same direction until well combined and sticky. Add both the oils and continue mixing until combined.

③ FILL AND FOLD THE DUMPLINGS

Divide the filling among the dumpling wrappers in 20 g (¾ oz) portions and fold following the instructions on page 10 or 11.

④ BOIL THE DUMPLINGS

Bring a large saucepan of water to the boil and add 15 dumplings. Wait for the water to come back up to the boil, then add 15 ml (½ fl oz) cold water. Repeat this process twice. While cooking, gently stir the dumplings to stop them sticking together. When they float to the surface, they are ready. Scoop out the dumplings with a slotted spoon and serve hot.

Cook the remaining dumplings in the same way.

Lamb & carrot

MAKES	30 DUMPLINGS
PREP	30 MINUTES
COOK	20 MINUTES

350 g (12½ oz) minced
(ground) lamb (20% fat
or higher)

250 g (1⅔ cups)
grated carrot

3 teaspoons finely chopped
fresh ginger

1¼ teaspoons sugar

1½ teaspoons salt

½ teaspoon ground
white pepper

½ teaspoon Chinese
five-spice

15 ml (½ fl oz) light soy sauce

100 ml (3½ fl oz) water

30 ml (1 fl oz) sesame oil

① PREPARE THE DOUGH

Prepare the dough following the instructions on page 8.

② PREPARE THE FILLING

Place the meat in a large bowl, breaking it up a bit with a wooden spoon or chopsticks. Add the remaining ingredients, except the sesame oil. Mix vigorously in the same direction until well combined and sticky. Add the sesame oil and continue mixing until combined.

③ FILL AND FOLD THE DUMPLINGS

Divide the filling among the dumpling wrappers in 20 g (¾ oz) portions and fold following the instructions on page 10 or 11.

④ BOIL THE DUMPLINGS

Bring a large saucepan of water to the boil and add 15 dumplings. Wait for the water to come back up to the boil, then add 15 ml (½ fl oz) cold water. Repeat this process twice. While cooking, gently stir the dumplings to stop them sticking together. When they float to the surface, they are ready. Scoop out the dumplings with a slotted spoon and serve hot.

Cook the remaining dumplings in the same way.

Vegetarian

MAKES 30 DUMPLINGS

PREP 30 MINUTES

COOK 20 MINUTES

4 eggs

20 ml (¾ fl oz) vegetable oil

pinch of salt

200 g (7 oz) vermicelli
rice noodles

200 g (7 oz) spring onions
(scallions), finely sliced

¾ teaspoon Chinese five-spice

1¾ teaspoons sugar

¾ teaspoon MSG

20 ml (¾ fl oz) sesame oil

1 PREPARE THE DOUGH

Prepare the dough following the instructions on page 8.

2 PREPARE THE FILLING

Whisk together the eggs, vegetable oil and salt. Lightly scramble the eggs in an oiled frying pan, then remove to a board and chop into smaller pieces.

Meanwhile, soak the vermicelli noodles in boiling water for 2 minutes.

Drain the noodles, chop into smaller pieces and add to a large bowl with the egg. Add the spring onion, five-spice, sugar and MSG. Stir together in the same direction, then add the sesame oil and mix until combined.

3 FILL AND FOLD THE DUMPLINGS

Divide the filling among the dumpling wrappers in 15 g (½ oz) portions and fold following the instructions on page 10 or 11.

4 BOIL THE DUMPLINGS

Bring a large saucepan of water to the boil and add 15 dumplings. Wait for the water to come back up to the boil, then add 15 ml (½ fl oz) cold water. Repeat this process twice. While cooking, gently stir the dumplings to stop them sticking together. When they float to the surface, they are ready. Scoop out the dumplings with a slotted spoon and serve hot.

Cook the remaining dumplings in the same way.

EAT IT WITH...

Vinegar sauce

30 ml (1 fl oz) black vinegar
1 teaspoon sesame oil

Combine the ingredients in a bowl. This sauce is typically served with all types of Chinese dumplings.

ZHAO's sauce

40 ml (1¼ fl oz) chilli oil
30 ml (1 fl oz) light soy sauce
15 ml (½ fl oz) black vinegar
1 teaspoon sesame oil
3½ teaspoons sugar
4 garlic cloves, finely chopped
2 tablespoons chopped chives

In a bowl, combine the chilli oil, soy sauce, vinegar and sesame oil. Add the sugar and mix until dissolved, then stir in the garlic and chives.

Pork & corn

MAKES 30 DUMPLINGS	
PREP 30 MINUTES	
COOK 12 MINUTES PER BATCH	

*350 g (12½ oz) minced
(ground) pork (semi lean)*

*20 ml (¾ fl oz) light
soy sauce*

20 ml (¾ fl oz) sesame oil

1½ teaspoons salt

*½ teaspoon ground
white pepper*

½ teaspoon MSG

100 ml (3½ fl oz) water

300 g (10½ oz) corn kernels

1 PREPARE THE DOUGH

Prepare the dough following the instructions on page 8.

2 PREPARE THE FILLING

Place the meat in a large bowl, breaking it up a bit with a wooden spoon or chopsticks. Add the remaining ingredients, except the corn. Mix vigorously in the same direction until well combined and sticky. Add the corn and continue to mix until well combined.

3 FILL AND FOLD THE DUMPLINGS

Divide the filling among the dumpling wrappers in 20 g (¾ oz) portions and fold following the instructions on page 10 or 11.

4 STEAM THE DUMPLINGS

Bring a saucepan of water to the boil. In batches, place the dumplings in a steamer basket, set the basket over the saucepan and steam for 12 minutes. Remove the dumplings and serve hot.

Cook the remaining dumplings in the same way.

Crystal prawn

MAKES 30 DUMPLINGS	
PREP 45 MINUTES	
REST 2 HOURS	
COOK 8 MINUTES PER BATCH	

Filling

500 g (1 lb 2 oz) raw prawns (shrimp)

15 g (½ oz) tinned bamboo shoots, rinsed and drained

2 egg whites

100 g (3½ oz) minced (ground) pork

1½ tablespoons sugar

3¼ teaspoons cornflour (cornstarch)

2 teaspoons salt

Dough

170 g (6 oz) cornflour (cornstarch)

90 g (3 oz) plain (all-purpose) flour

260 ml (9 fl oz) boiling water

2¼ teaspoons sugar

2 teaspoons vegetable oil

For cooking

chilli oil

1 PREPARE THE FILLING

Peel and devein the prawns. Rinse them clean, then pat dry with paper towel. Using a sharp knife, chop them very finely and set aside.

Finely chop the bamboo shoots and set aside.

Place the egg whites in a large bowl. Add the pork and break it up a bit with a wooden spoon. Add the remaining filling ingredients and mix well until combined and sticky.

Cover with plastic wrap and refrigerate for 2 hours.

2 PREPARE THE DOUGH

In a large mixing bowl, combine the cornflour and half the plain flour. Pour in the boiling water and stir, then cover with plastic wrap for 2 minutes.

Add the remaining flour, sugar and oil and knead until the dough is smooth. Roll the dough into a long strip and cut into 10 g (¼ oz) pieces.

3 FILL AND FOLD THE DUMPLINGS

Roll out the dough pieces into rounds using a rolling pin. Divide the filling among the dumpling wrappers in 20 g (¾ oz) portions and fold following the instructions on page 10 or 11.

4 STEAM THE DUMPLINGS

Bring a saucepan of water to the boil. In batches, place the dumplings in a steamer basket, adding a little chilli oil. Set the basket over the saucepan and steam for 8 minutes. Remove the dumplings and serve hot.

Cook the remaining dumplings in the same way.

Seafood

MAKES 30 DUMPLINGS

PREP 30 MINUTES

COOK 12 MINUTES PER BATCH

500 g (1 lb 2 oz) firm white fish fillets

100 g (3½ oz) peeled raw prawns (shrimp)

1 egg white

20 g (⅓ cup) finely chopped chives

2 teaspoons finely chopped fresh ginger

3¼ teaspoons cornflour (cornstarch)

2½ teaspoons sugar

1¾ teaspoons salt

½ teaspoon ground white pepper

½ teaspoon MSG

2 teaspoons sesame oil

50 ml (1¾ fl oz) water

① PREPARE THE DOUGH

Prepare the dough following the instructions on page 8.

② PREPARE THE FILLING

Finely chop the fish and prawns, then place in a large bowl with the remaining ingredients. Mix vigorously in the same direction until well combined and sticky.

③ FILL AND FOLD THE DUMPLINGS

Divide the filling among the dumpling wrappers in 20 g (¾ oz) portions and fold following the instructions on page 10 or 11.

④ STEAM THE DUMPLINGS

Bring a saucepan of water to the boil. In batches, place the dumplings in a steamer basket, set the basket over the saucepan and steam for 12 minutes. Remove the dumplings and serve hot.

Cook the remaining dumplings in the same way.

Four-flavour

MAKES 30 DUMPLINGS

PREP 30 MINUTES

COOK 12 MINUTES PER BATCH

Filling

400 g (14 oz) all-purpose potatoes (for mashing)

80 g (2¾ oz) butter, softened

1¼ teaspoons salt

½ teaspoon ground black pepper

30 g (⅔ cup) finely chopped chives

Toppings

60 g (2 oz) fresh Chinese black fungus, chopped

60 g (2 oz) corn kernels

60 g (2 oz) finely diced carrot

60 g (2 oz) finely diced celery

1 PREPARE THE DOUGH

Prepare the dough following the instructions on page 8.

2 PREPARE THE FILLING

Peel and halve the potatoes. Place them in a large saucepan, fill with cold water, bring to the boil and cook for 20 minutes, or until soft. Remove from the heat and drain off the water. Mash the potatoes, then add the remaining filling ingredients and mix well.

3 FILL AND FOLD THE DUMPLINGS

Divide the filling among the dumpling wrappers in 15 g (½ oz) portions and fold following the instructions on page 13. Place one of each vegetable topping into the four openings.

4 STEAM THE DUMPLINGS

Bring a saucepan of water to the boil. In batches, place the dumplings in a steamer basket, set the basket over the saucepan and steam for 12 minutes. Remove the dumplings and serve hot.

Cook the remaining dumplings in the same way.

Beef

MAKES 30 DUMPLINGS	
PREP 30 MINUTES	
COOK 12 MINUTES PER BATCH	

550 g (1 lb 3 oz) minced (ground) beef (20% fat or higher)

60 g (scant 1¼ cup) finely chopped chives

4 teaspoons finely chopped fresh ginger

20 ml (¾ fl oz) light soy sauce

2½ teaspoons sugar

2 teaspoons salt

1¼ teaspoons MSG

½ teaspoon Chinese five-spice

100 ml (3½ fl oz) water

30 ml (1 fl oz) sesame oil

1 **PREPARE THE DOUGH**

Prepare the dough following the instructions on page 8.

2 **PREPARE THE FILLING**

Place the meat in a large bowl, breaking it up a bit with a wooden spoon or chopsticks. Add the remaining ingredients, except the sesame oil. Mix vigorously in the same direction until sticky. Add the sesame oil and mix until well combined.

3 **FILL AND FOLD THE DUMPLINGS**

Divide the filling among the dumpling wrappers in 20 g (¾ oz) portions and fold following the instructions on page 10 or 11.

4 **STEAM THE DUMPLINGS**

Bring a saucepan of water to the boil. In batches, place the dumplings in a steamer basket, set the basket over the saucepan and steam for 12 minutes. Remove the dumplings and serve hot.
    Cook the remaining dumplings in the same way.

Chicken

MAKES 30 DUMPLINGS	
PREP 30 MINUTES	
COOK 12 MINUTES PER BATCH	

400 g (14 oz) minced (ground) chicken

30 g (⅔ cup) finely chopped chives

2 teaspoons finely chopped fresh ginger

2 teaspoons light soy sauce

1¾ teaspoons sugar

1½ teaspoons salt

¾ teaspoon chicken stock powder

50 ml (1¾ fl oz) water

250 g (9 oz) cabbage, chopped

20 ml (¾ fl oz) sesame oil

1 PREPARE THE DOUGH

Prepare the dough following the instructions on page 8.

2 PREPARE THE FILLING

Place the meat in a large bowl, breaking it up a bit with a wooden spoon or chopsticks. Add the remaining ingredients, except the cabbage and sesame oil. Mix to combine, then add the cabbage. Mix vigorously in the same direction until sticky. Add the sesame oil and mix until well combined.

3 FILL AND FOLD THE DUMPLINGS

Divide the filling among the dumpling wrappers in 20 g (¾ oz) portions and fold following the instructions on page 10 or 11.

4 STEAM THE DUMPLINGS

Bring a saucepan of water to the boil. In batches, place the dumplings in a steamer basket, set the basket over the saucepan and steam for 12 minutes. Remove the dumplings and serve hot.

Cook the remaining dumplings in the same way.

Dumplings

Noun

Appearing more than 1800 years ago during the Han dynasty, dumplings – or jiaozi (餃子) in Chinese – are said to have been created by the doctor Zhang Zhongjing. Dumplings can be steamed using a bamboo steam basket, boiled, pan-fried, or even served in soup. On their own, they are often served with a spicy dipping sauce.

Henan

MAKES 30 DUMPLINGS

PREP 30 MINUTES

COOK 8 MINUTES PER BATCH

---

400 g (14 oz) minced (ground) pork (semi-lean)

250 g (9 oz) leeks, white part only, finely sliced

1½ teaspoons salt

1¼ teaspoons sugar

1¼ teaspoons MSG

¾ teaspoon Chinese five-spice

½ teaspoon ground white pepper

20 ml (¾ fl oz) sesame oil

15 ml (½ fl oz) light soy sauce

50 ml (1¾ fl oz) water

For cooking

30 ml (1 fl oz) cooking oil (per batch)

1 PREPARE THE DOUGH

Prepare the dough following the instructions on page 8.

2 PREPARE THE FILLING

Place the meat in a large bowl, breaking it up a bit with a wooden spoon or chopsticks. Add the remaining ingredients. Mix vigorously in the same direction until well combined and sticky.

3 FILL AND FOLD THE DUMPLINGS

Divide the filling among the dumpling wrappers in 15 g (½ oz) portions. Fold and pinch two opposite edges of each wrapper together, leaving the top and bottom ends of the dumpling open.

4 PAN-FRY THE DUMPLINGS

Heat a large frying pan over medium heat. Add the oil and, in batches, fry the dumplings for 4–5 minutes.

Add about 30 ml (1 fl oz) water to the pan, cover the pan with a lid and cook over low heat for a further 3 minutes. Remove the dumplings and serve hot.

Cook the remaining dumplings in the same way.

Shanghai

MAKES 30 DUMPLINGS	
PREP 30 MINUTES	
COOK 8 MINUTES PER BATCH	

600 g (1 lb 5 oz) minced (ground) pork (semi-lean)

2 eggs

4 teaspoons finely chopped fresh ginger

2 teaspoons sugar

1¾ teaspoons salt

1½ teaspoons ground white pepper

40 ml (1¼ fl oz) light soy sauce

20 ml (¾ fl oz) sesame oil

20 ml (¾ fl oz) vegetable oil

60 ml (¼ cup) water

For cooking

30 ml (1 fl oz) cooking oil (per batch)

① PREPARE THE DOUGH

Prepare the dough following the instructions on page 8.

② PREPARE THE FILLING

Place the meat in a large bowl, breaking it up a bit with a wooden spoon or chopsticks. Add the remaining ingredients. Mix vigorously in the same direction until well combined and sticky.

③ FILL AND FOLD THE DUMPLINGS

Divide the filling among the dumpling wrappers in 15 g (½ oz) portions and fold following the instructions on page 10 or 11.

④ PAN-FRY THE DUMPLINGS

Heat a large frying pan over medium heat. Add the oil and, in batches, fry the dumplings for 4–5 minutes.

Add about 30 ml (1 fl oz) water to the pan, cover the pan with a lid and cook over low heat for a further 3 minutes. Remove the dumplings and serve hot.

Cook the remaining dumplings in the same way.

Nanjing

400 g minced (ground) beef
(20% fat or higher)

300 g (2 cups) finely diced
onion

60 g (2 oz) finely chopped
chives

4 teaspoons finely chopped
fresh ginger

2½ teaspoons sugar

1½ teaspoons salt

1¼ teaspoons MSG

¾ teaspoon Chinese
five-spice

½ teaspoon ground
white pepper

30 ml (1 fl oz) Chinese
cooking wine

50 ml (1¾ fl oz) water

20 ml (¾ fl oz) sesame oil

For cooking

30 ml (1 fl oz) cooking oil
(per batch)

① PREPARE THE DOUGH

Prepare the dough following the instructions on page 8.

② PREPARE THE FILLING

Place the meat in a large bowl, breaking it up a bit with a wooden spoon or chopsticks. Add the remaining ingredients, except the sesame oil. Mix vigorously in the same direction until the mixture becomes sticky, then add the sesame oil and mix until combined.

③ FILL AND FOLD THE DUMPLINGS

Divide the filling among the dumpling wrappers in 15 g (½ oz) portions. Fold following the instructions on page 10 or 11, aiming for an elongated crescent shape.

④ PAN-FRY THE DUMPLINGS

Heat a large frying pan over medium heat. Add the oil and, in batches, fry the dumplings for 4–5 minutes.
Add about 30 ml (1 fl oz) water to the pan, cover the pan with a lid and cook over low heat for a further 3 minutes. Remove the dumplings and serve hot.
Cook the remaining dumplings in the same way.

Golden Fish

MAKES 30 DUMPLINGS	
PREP 30 MINUTES	
COOK 8 MINUTES PER BATCH	

500 g (1 lb 2 oz) firm white fish fillets

140 g (1 cup) finely chopped celery

4 teaspoons finely chopped fresh ginger

1 egg white

1½ teaspoons cornflour (cornstarch)

1½ teaspoons salt

1¼ teaspoons sugar

¾ teaspoon MSG

½ teaspoon ground white pepper

2 teaspoons sesame oil

For cooking

30 ml (1 fl oz) cooking oil (per batch)

1 PREPARE THE DOUGH

Prepare the dough following the instructions on page 8.

2 PREPARE THE FILLING

Finely chop the fish. Place in a large bowl and add the remaining ingredients, except the sesame oil. Mix vigorously in the same direction until the mixture becomes sticky, then add the sesame oil and mix until combined.

3 FILL AND FOLD THE DUMPLINGS

Divide the filling among the dumpling wrappers in 20 g (¾ oz) portions and fold following the instructions on page 10 or 11.

4 PAN-FRY THE DUMPLINGS

Heat a large frying pan over medium heat. Add the oil and, in batches, fry the dumplings for 4–5 minutes.

Add about 30 ml (1 fl oz) water to the pan, cover the pan with a lid and cook over low heat for a further 3 minutes. Remove the dumplings and serve hot.

Cook the remaining dumplings in the same way.

Cabbage & tofu

MAKES 30 DUMPLINGS	
PREP 30 MINUTES	
COOK 8 MINUTES PER BATCH	

400 g (14 oz) cabbage, finely chopped

100 g (⅔ cup) grated carrot

50 g (1¾ oz) fried tofu, finely chopped

3 teaspoons salt

2½ teaspoons sugar

1¼ teaspoons MSG

¾ teaspoon ground white pepper

20 ml (¾ fl oz) sesame oil

For cooking

30 ml (1 fl oz) cooking oil (per batch)

① PREPARE THE DOUGH

Prepare the dough following the instructions on page 8.

② PREPARE THE FILLING

Place the vegetables and tofu in a large bowl. Add the remaining ingredients, except the sesame oil. Mix vigorously in the same direction until the mixture becomes sticky, then add the sesame oil and mix until combined.

③ FILL AND FOLD THE DUMPLINGS

Divide the filling among the dumpling wrappers in 20 g (¾ oz) portions and fold following the instructions on page 10 or 11.

④ PAN-FRY THE DUMPLINGS

Heat a large frying pan over medium heat. Add the oil and, in batches, fry the dumplings for 4—5 minutes.

Add about 30 ml (1 fl oz) water to the pan, cover the pan with a lid and cook over low heat for a further 3 minutes. Remove the dumplings and serve hot.

Cook the remaining dumplings in the same way.

Pork & prawn

MAKES 30 DUMPLINGS

PREP 30 MINUTES

COOK 8 MINUTES PER BATCH

350 g (12½ oz) minced (ground) pork (semi-lean)

150 g (5½ oz) raw prawns (shrimp), peeled and deveined, then finely chopped

4 teaspoons finely chopped fresh ginger

15 ml (½ fl oz) light soy sauce

2 teaspoons salt

1¾ teaspoons sugar

1¼ teaspoons MSG

½ teaspoon ground white pepper

100 g (3½ oz) spring onions (scallions), finely sliced

20 ml (¾ fl oz) sesame oil

For cooking

30 ml (1 fl oz) cooking oil (per batch)

1 PREPARE THE DOUGH

Prepare the dough following the instructions on page 8.

2 PREPARE THE FILLING

Place the meat in a large bowl, breaking it up a bit with a wooden spoon or chopsticks. Add the remaining ingredients, except the spring onion and sesame oil. Mix vigorously in the same direction until the mixture becomes sticky. Mix the spring onion through. Add the sesame oil and mix until combined.

3 FILL AND FOLD THE DUMPLINGS

Divide the filling among the dumpling wrappers in 20 g (¾ oz) portions and fold following the instructions on page 10 or 11.

4 PAN-FRY THE DUMPLINGS

Heat a large frying pan over medium heat. Add the oil and, in batches, fry the dumplings for 4–5 minutes.

Add about 30 ml (1 fl oz) water to the pan, cover the pan with a lid and cook over low heat for a further 3 minutes. Remove the dumplings and serve hot.

Cook the remaining dumplings in the same way.

ZHAO'S PANTRY

Chilli oil

Chinese five-spice

Black vinegar

Sweet soy sauce

Light soy sauce

Plain (all-purpose) flour

Chicken stock
powder

Egg dumpling soup

SERVES 1 + EXTRA DUMPLINGS

PREP 35 MINUTES

COOK 30 MINUTES

Egg batter

6 eggs

1¼ teaspoons cornflour
(cornstarch)

20 ml (¾ fl oz) water

Filling

250 g (9 oz) minced (ground)
pork (semi-lean)

40 g (¾ cup) finely chopped
chives

2 teaspoons finely chopped
fresh ginger

2 teaspoons light soy sauce

2 teaspoons sesame oil

1¼ teaspoons sugar

1 teaspoon salt

½ teaspoon ground white pepper

Soup

1–2 tablespoons dried shrimp

1 nori sheet, torn

1 teaspoon salt

¾ teaspoon chicken stock powder
(optional)

½ teaspoon light soy sauce

½ teaspoon sesame oil

1 PREPARE THE EGG BATTER

Crack the eggs into a bowl and whisk thoroughly.
In a small bowl, whisk the cornflour and water to
make a thin slurry. Add the slurry to the eggs and
mix until well combined. Set aside.

2 PREPARE THE FILLING

Place the meat in a large bowl, breaking it up a
bit with a wooden spoon or chopsticks. Add the
remaining filling ingredients. Mix vigorously in the
same direction until well combined and sticky.

3 MAKE THE DUMPLINGS

Warm a non-stick frying pan over low heat. Add
about 12 g (½ oz) of the egg batter and swirl the
pan to spread it into a thin circle. Add 8 g (¼ oz) of
filling to the centre and use a spatula to fold the egg
wrapper in half. Remove from the pan and cook the
remaining dumplings in the same way.

4 MAKE THE SOUP

Bring a large saucepan of water to the boil. Add
15 dumplings and 50 ml (1¾ fl oz) cold water and
gently stir to stop the dumplings sticking to one
another. When they float to the surface, remove
with a slotted spoon and cook the remaining
dumplings in the same way.

In another saucepan, bring 250 ml (1 cup) water
to the boil. Add the soup ingredients and return to
the boil. Add the dumplings and cook over medium
heat for 2 minutes.

Transfer to a serving bowl and serve hot.

Shaanxi dumpling soup

SERVES 1 + EXTRA DUMPLINGS

PREP 35 MINUTES

COOK 30 MINUTES

Filling

600 g (1 lb 5 oz) minced (ground) pork (semi-lean)

60 g (2 oz) finely chopped chives

4 teaspoons finely chopped fresh ginger

2½ teaspoons sugar

2 teaspoons salt

½ teaspoon Chinese five-spice

20 ml (¾ fl oz) light soy sauce

50 ml (1¾ fl oz) water

Soup

1–2 tablespoons dried shrimp

1¼ teaspoons chicken stock powder

1 teaspoon light soy sauce

1 teaspoon black vinegar

¼ teaspoon sesame oil

To garnish

chopped coriander (cilantro)

chopped chives

chilli oil

1 PREPARE THE DOUGH

Prepare the dough following the instructions on page 8.

2 PREPARE THE FILLING

Place the meat in a large bowl, breaking it up a bit with a wooden spoon or chopsticks. Add the remaining filling ingredients. Mix vigorously in the same direction until well combined and sticky.

3 FILL AND FOLD THE DUMPLINGS

Divide the filling among the dumpling wrappers in 20 g (¾ oz) portions and fold following the instructions on page 12.

4 MAKE THE SOUP

Bring a large saucepan of water to the boil. Add 15 dumplings and 50 ml (1¾ fl oz) cold water and gently stir to stop the dumplings sticking to one another. When they float to the surface, remove with a slotted spoon and cook the remaining dumplings in the same way.

In another saucepan, bring 250 ml (1 cup) water to the boil. Add the soup ingredients and return to the boil. Turn off the heat and add the dumplings.

Transfer to a serving bowl, finish with the herbs and a drizzle of chilli oil and serve hot.

liáo zà liè

撩咋咧

Tiny dumpling soup

SERVES 1 + EXTRA DUMPLINGS

PREP 35 MINUTES

COOK 30 MINUTES

Filling

200 g (7 oz) minced (ground)
pork (semi-lean)

80 g (2¾ oz) shiitake
mushrooms, finely chopped

2 teaspoons finely chopped
fresh ginger

1 teaspoon sugar

¾ teaspoon salt

½ teaspoon chicken
stock powder

½ teaspoon ground
white pepper

50 ml (1¾ fl oz) water

Soup

1 bunch of choy sum, chopped

1¼ teaspoons chicken
stock powder

½ teaspoon sesame oil

To garnish

chopped coriander (cilantro)

chopped chives

1 **PREPARE THE DOUGH**

Prepare and rest the dough following the
instructions on page 8, but don't roll it out just yet.

2 **PREPARE THE FILLING**

Place the meat in a large bowl, breaking it up a
bit with a wooden spoon or chopsticks. Add the
remaining filling ingredients. Mix vigorously in the
same direction until well combined and sticky.

3 **FILL AND FOLD THE DUMPLINGS**

Roll the dumpling dough into long strips. Cut into
5 g (¼ oz) pieces and roll out into discs.

Divide the filling among the wrappers in 8 g
(¼ oz) portions and fold following the instructions
on page 12.

4 **MAKE THE SOUP**

Bring a large saucepan of water to the boil. Add
15 dumplings and 50 ml (1¾ fl oz) cold water and
gently stir to stop the dumplings sticking to one
another. When they float to the surface, remove
with a slotted spoon and cook the remaining
dumplings in the same way.

In another saucepan, bring 250 ml (1 cup) water
to the boil. Add the soup ingredients and return to
the boil. Turn off the heat and add the dumplings.

Transfer to a serving bowl, top with the
chopped herbs and serve hot.

Vegetable dumpling soup

SERVES 1 + EXTRA DUMPLINGS	
PREP 35 MINUTES	
COOK 30 MINUTES	

Filling

300 g (10½ oz) extra-firm tofu,
finely chopped

150 g (5½ oz) Chinese cabbage,
chopped

80 g (½ cup) finely diced carrot

70 g (2½ oz) fresh Chinese black
fungus, finely chopped

3 teaspoons salt

2½ teaspoons sugar

½ teaspoon MSG

20 ml (¾ fl oz) sesame oil

Soup

1 bok choy, ends removed

3–4 mushrooms, sliced

200 g (7 oz) tinned
diced tomatoes

¾ teaspoon sugar

½ teaspoon ground white pepper

¼ teaspoon MSG

½ teaspoon sesame oil

To garnish

chopped chives

① PREPARE THE DOUGH

Prepare the dough following the instructions on page 8.

② PREPARE THE FILLING

Place all the filling ingredients, except the sesame oil, in a large bowl. Mix vigorously in the same direction, then add the sesame oil and mix until combined.

③ FILL AND FOLD THE DUMPLINGS

Divide the filling among the dumpling wrappers in 20 g (¾ oz) portions and fold following the instructions on page 12.

④ MAKE THE SOUP

Bring a large saucepan of water to the boil. Add 15 dumplings and 50 ml (1¾ fl oz) cold water and gently stir to stop the dumplings sticking to one another. When they float to the surface, remove with a slotted spoon and cook the remaining dumplings in the same way.

In another saucepan, bring 250 ml (1 cup) water to the boil. Add the soup ingredients, return to the boil and cook for 3 minutes. Turn off the heat and add the dumplings.

Transfer to a serving bowl, top with chopped chives and serve hot.

Beef dumpling soup

SERVES 1 + EXTRA DUMPLINGS	
PREP 35 MINUTES	
COOK 30 MINUTES	

Filling

400 g (14 oz) minced (ground) beef (20% fat or higher)

210 g (1½ cups) finely chopped celery

2 teaspoons salt

2 teaspoons sugar

1¼ teaspoons MSG

¾ teaspoon Chinese five-spice

½ teaspoon ground white pepper

3 teaspoons light soy sauce

2 teaspoons oyster sauce

30 ml (1 fl oz) sesame oil

Soup

1 beef stock cube

2 teaspoons light soy sauce

¾ teaspoon MSG

½ teaspoon sesame oil

To garnish

chopped chives

chopped coriander (cilantro)

chilli oil

1 PREPARE THE DOUGH

Prepare the dough following the instructions on page 8.

2 PREPARE THE FILLING

Place the meat in a large bowl, breaking it up a bit with a wooden spoon or chopsticks. Add the remaining filling ingredients, except the sesame oil. Mix vigorously in the same direction until sticky, then add the sesame oil and mix until combined.

3 FILL AND FOLD THE DUMPLINGS

Divide the filling among the dumpling wrappers in 20 g (¾ oz) portions and fold following the instructions on page 10.

4 MAKE THE SOUP

Bring a large saucepan of water to the boil. Add 15 dumplings and 50 ml (1¾ fl oz) cold water and gently stir to stop the dumplings sticking to one another. When they float to the surface, remove with a slotted spoon and cook the remaining dumplings in the same way.

In another saucepan, bring 250 ml (1 cup) water to the boil. Add the stock cube and stir until dissolved, then add the remaining soup ingredients and return to the boil. Turn the heat off and add the dumplings.

Transfer to a serving bowl, finish with the herbs and a drizzle of chilli oil and serve hot.

First published in French by Hachette Livre (Marabout) in 2024
Hachette Book 58, rue Jean-Bleuzen 92178 Vanves Cedex

This edition published in 2025 by Smith Street Books
Naarm (Melbourne) | Australia
smithstreetbooks.com

ISBN: 978-1-9230-4978-9

Smith Street Books respectfully acknowledges the Wurundjeri People of the Kulin Nation,
who are the Traditional Owners of the land on which we work, and we pay our respects to
their Elders past and present.

The moral right of the author has been asserted.

Thank you to Chan Pochuan and Zhu Xi for providing the recipes.

For Hachette Livre (Marabout)
Proofreading: Emilie Collet
Layout: Jérôme Cousin, NoOok
Recipes: Chan Pochuan and Zhu Xi
Illustrations: Valentine Ferrandi

For Smith Street Books
Publisher: Paul McNally
Project editor and translator: Lucy Grant
Editor: Katri Hilden
Proofreader: Pam Dunne

Printed & bound in China
Book 365
10 9 8 7 6 5 4 3 2 1